JUSTIN TIMBERLAKE

PIANO VOCAL GUITAR

Man of the Woods

ISBN 978-1-5400-2437-4

7777 W. BLUEMOUND RD. P.O. BOX 13819 MILWAUKEE, WI 53213

Visit Hal Leonard Online at
www.halleonard.com

FILTHY

Words and Music by JUSTIN TIMBERLAKE,
JAMES FAUNTLEROY, NATE HILLS,
LARRANCE DOPSON and TIMOTHY MOSLEY

Moderate Techno Pop

* Recorded a half step higher.

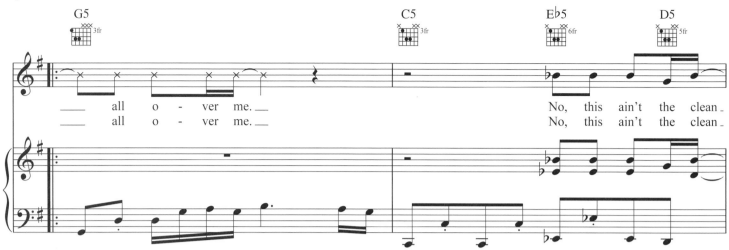

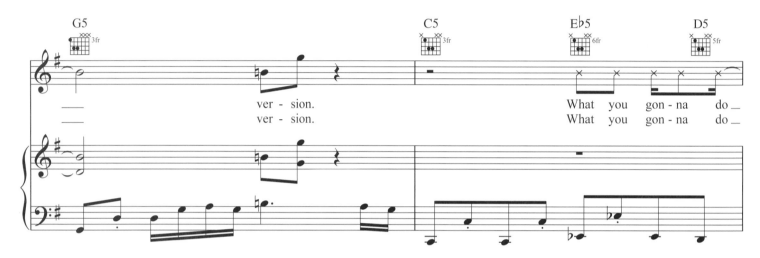

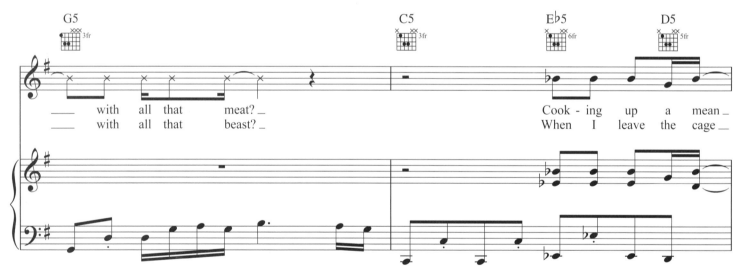

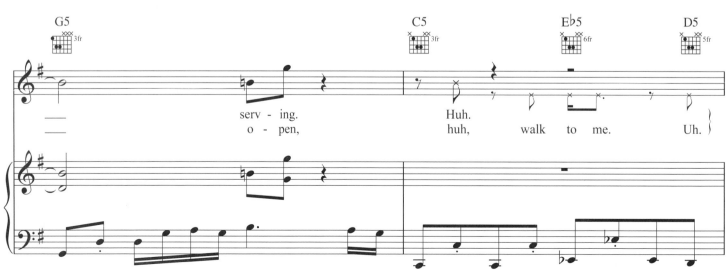

No ques - tion, I want it. Fire up, ev - 'ry - bod - y smok - ing.

Your friends, my friends, and they ain't leav - ing 'til six in the morn - ing.

Caught a chill, ba - by, you're the cold - est. Go far, put 'em on no - tice.

If you know what I want, then ___ yeah. Ba - by, don't you

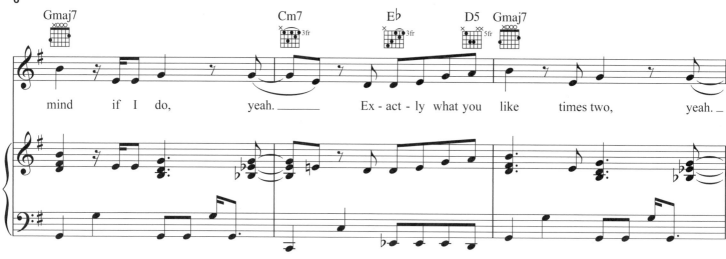

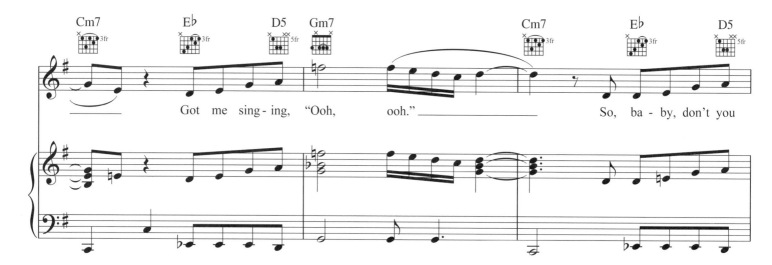

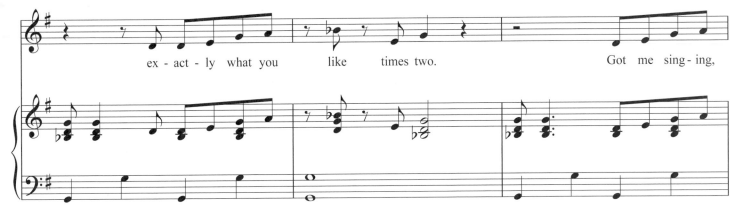

ex - act - ly what you like times two. Got me sing - ing,

"Ooh, ooh." ___ Ba - by, don't you mind if I do.

Come on, __ huh. Your friends, my friends, and they ain't leav - ing 'til six in the morn - ing.

Your friends, my friends, and

MIDNIGHT SUMMER JAM

Words and Music by JUSTIN TIMBERLAKE,
CHAD HUGO and PHARRELL WILLIAMS

Act like the South ain't the shit. Wait. It's just __ a mid - night sum - mer's jam. __

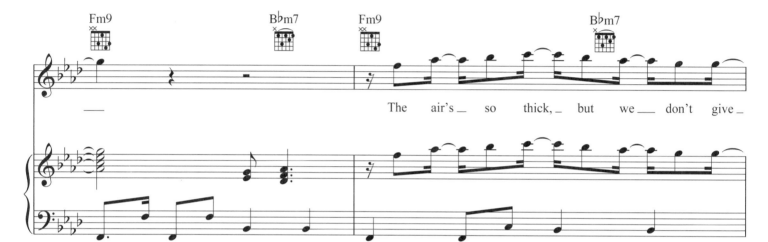

__ The air's __ so thick, __ but we __ don't give __

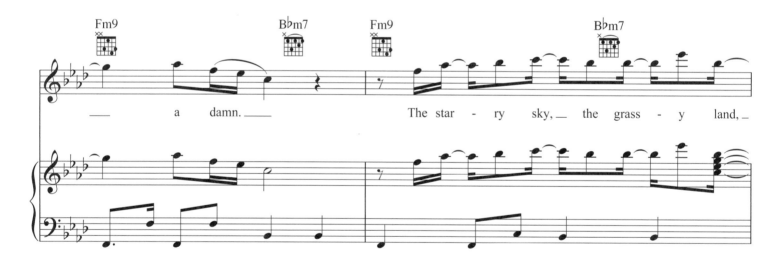

__ a damn. __ The star - ry sky, __ the grass - y land, __

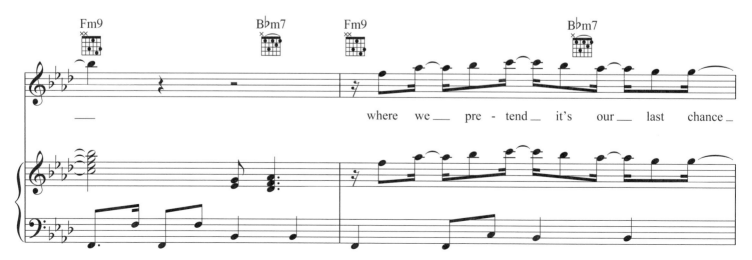

__ where we __ pre - tend __ it's our __ last chance __

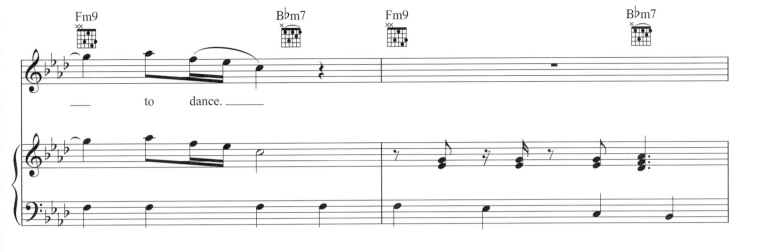

to dance. _____

It starts _ at mid - night, mid - night,   mid - night.

It starts _ at mid - night, mid - night,   mid - night.

It starts _ at mid - night, mid - night,   mid - night.

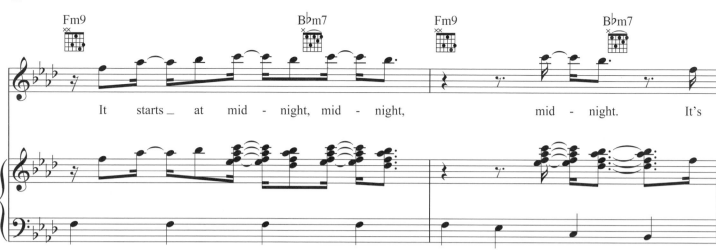

It starts __ at mid-night, mid-night, mid-night. It's

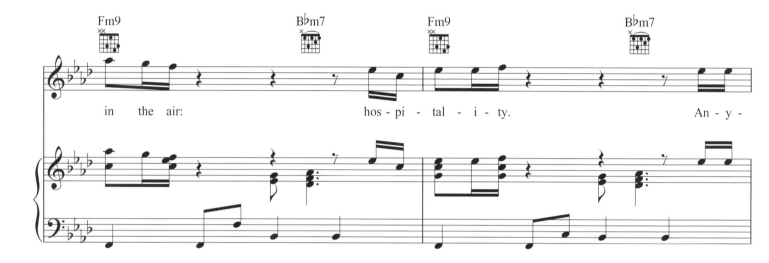

in the air: hos-pi-tal-i-ty. An-y-

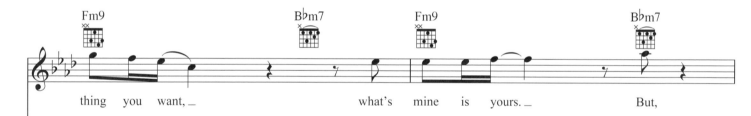

thing you want, __ what's mine is yours. __ But,

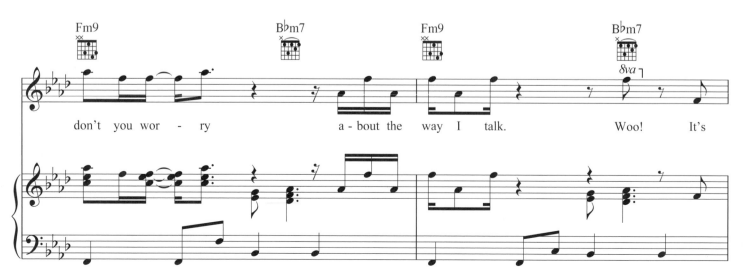

don't you wor-ry a-bout the way I talk. Woo! It's

where I'm from. _ Come and get you some. _ Uh.

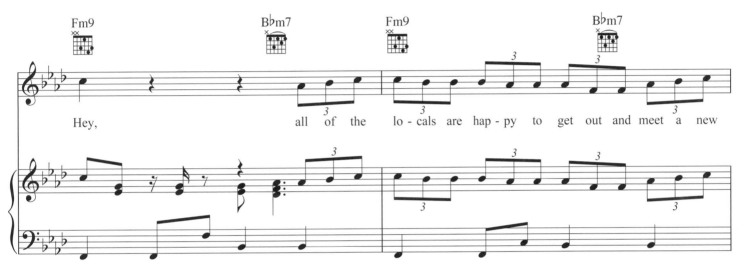

Hey, all of the lo - cals are hap - py to get out and meet a new

face. We dance in cir - cles on and on and do - sey - do, and then we

sway. E - ven the old folks will come out and rock, and we just

hop-ing the mu-sic don't stop till the next day. It's just _ a mid-night sum-mer's jam. _

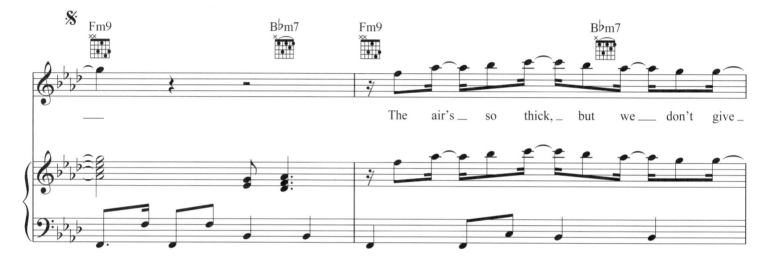

_ The air's _ so thick, _ but we _ don't give _

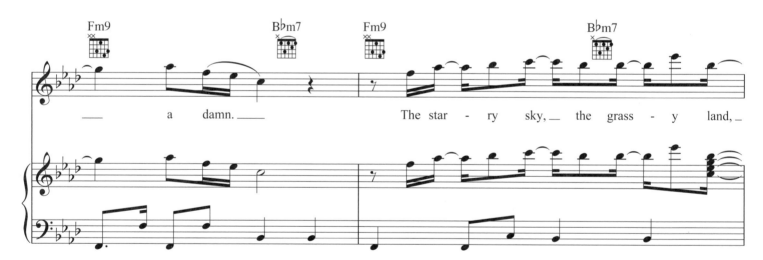

_ a damn. _ The star-ry sky, _ the grass-y land, _

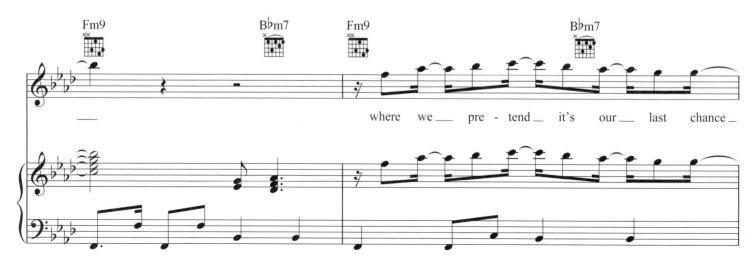

_ where we _ pre-tend _ it's our _ last chance _

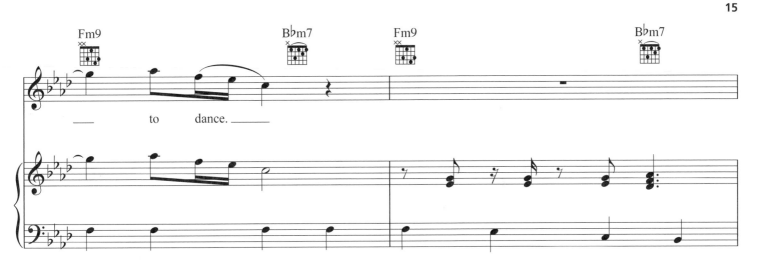

to dance.

It starts __ at mid - night, mid - night, __ mid - night.

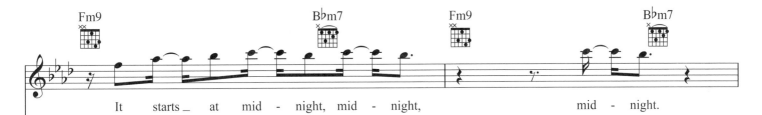

It starts __ at mid - night, mid - night, __ mid - night.

It starts __ at mid - night, mid - night, __ mid - night.

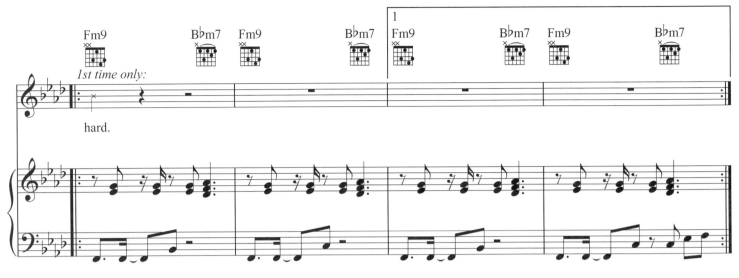

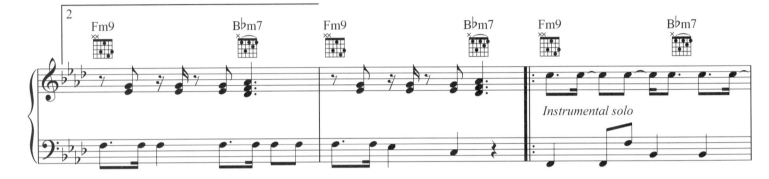

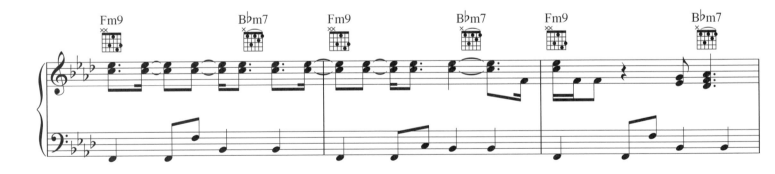

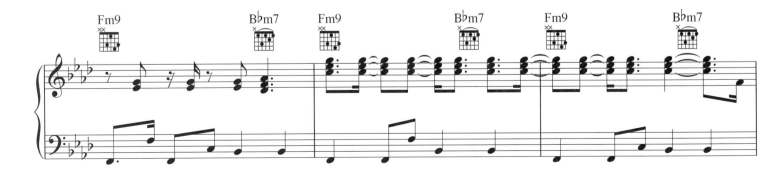

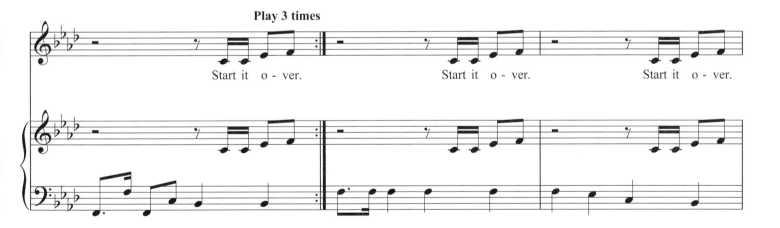

SAUCE

Words and Music by JUSTIN TIMBERLAKE,
NATE HILLS, ELLIOTT IVES
and TIMOTHY MOSELY

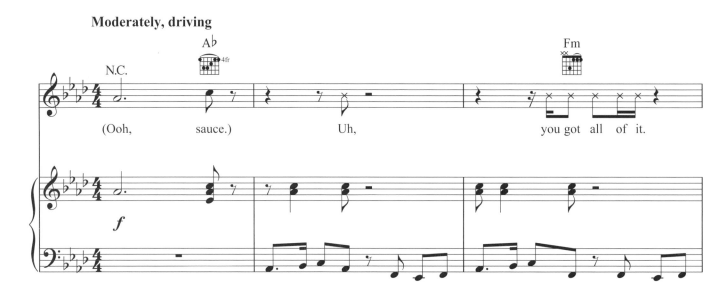

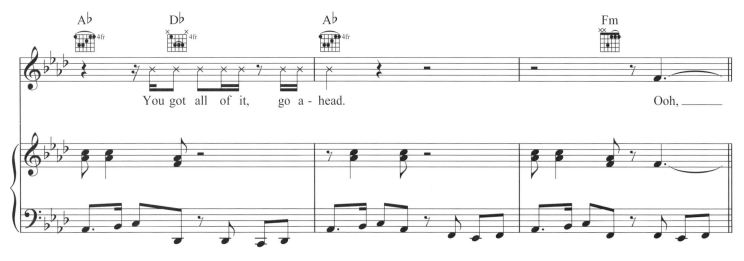

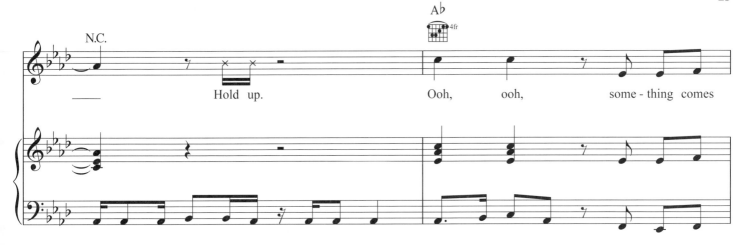

Hold up.　Ooh,　ooh,　some - thing comes

o - ver me.　It's all these loose screws when you get

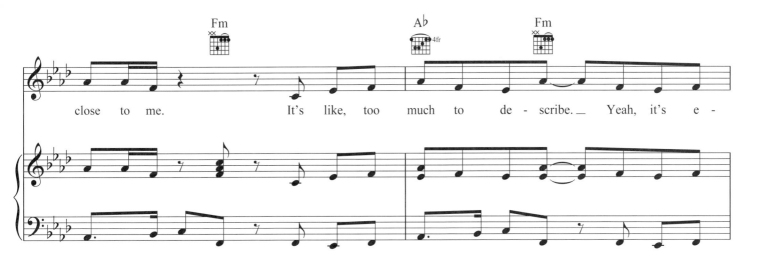

close to me.　It's like, too much to de - scribe.__ Yeah, it's e -

nough for two lives __ and I could nev - er spend all of it, but at

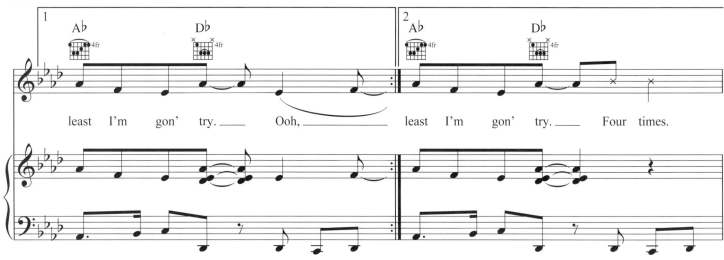

least I'm gon' try. ___ Ooh, _____ least I'm gon' try. ___ Four times.

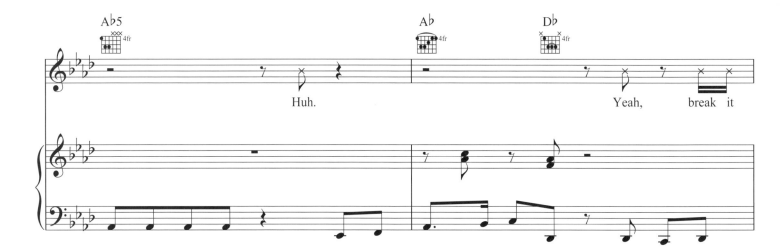

Huh.   Yeah,   break it

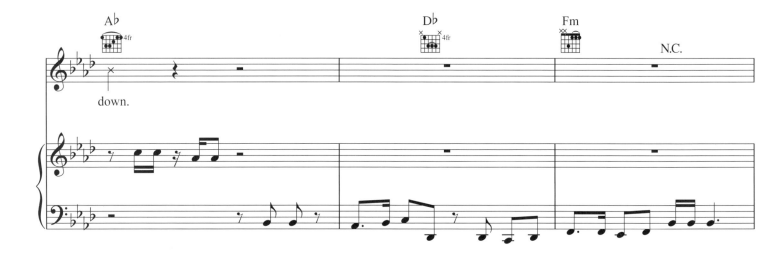

down.

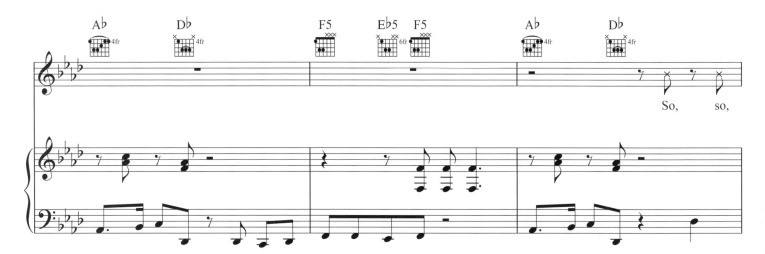

So,   so,

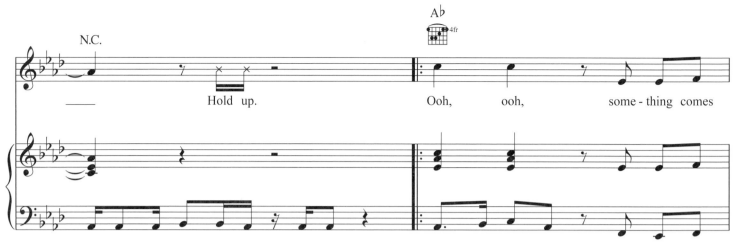

(Ooh, sauce.) Go 'head, _ you got all of it. Huh.

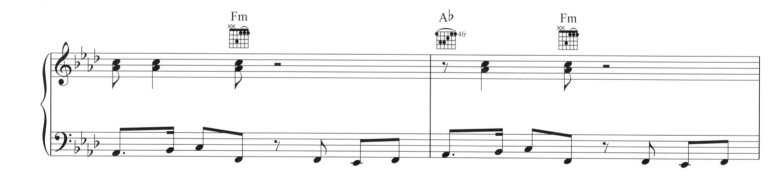

MAN OF THE WOODS

Words and Music by JUSTIN TIMBERLAKE,
CHAD HUGO and PHARRELL WILLIAMS

_____ you to an-y-one out-side, _____ but I'm a

man of _____ the woods, it's _____ my pride. _____ I'm sor-ry, ba-

To Coda

- by, you know _ I try, _____ but I'm a man of _____ the woods, it's _____ my

pride. _____ Well, _____ I got yours sweet with a twist of lime, _ and

side, _____ but I'm a man of ___ the woods, it's ___ my

pride. ___ I'm sor-ry, ba - by, ooh __ you know __ I try, _____ but I'm a

man of ___ the woods, it's ___ my pride. ___ Mm, __ I wrote this to let you know,

and I let them feel-ings show. I'm a man of ___ the woods, and you're ___ my

HIGHER HIGHER

Words and Music by JUSTIN TIMBERLAKE,
CHAD HUGO and PHARRELL WILLIAMS

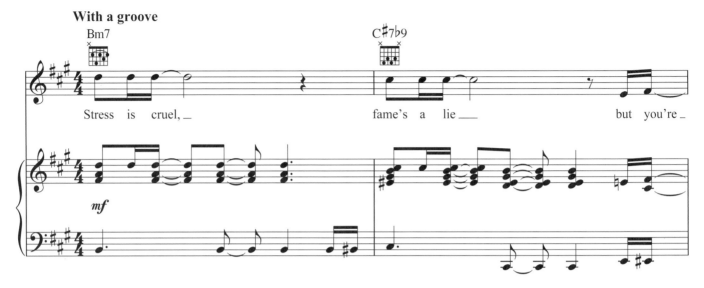

With a groove

Stress is cruel, _ fame's a lie _ but you're _

_ spe-cial on ev-'ry _ lev-el. Suc-cess is cool, _

mon-ey is fine _ but you're _ spe-cial, an-oth-er _

lev-el. Suc-cess is cool ___ and

mon-ey is fine ___ but you're _ spe-cial, an-oth-er ___ lev-el.

I guess you can say I was love - struck. I met you, you was with your broth - er.

I had to go and get my cous - in, tell a joke and then say, "What's _ up?"

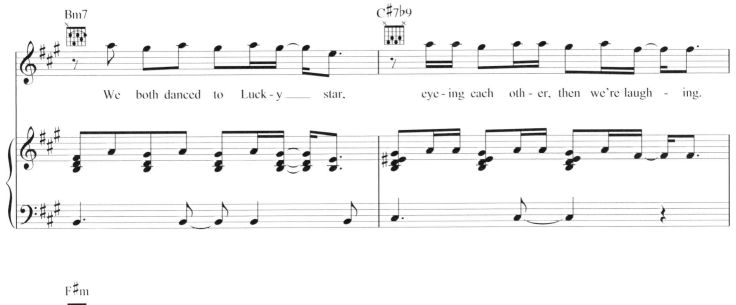

it's for you,＿ can't be an-y old thing. If it's for you,＿ can't be an-y old thing. If

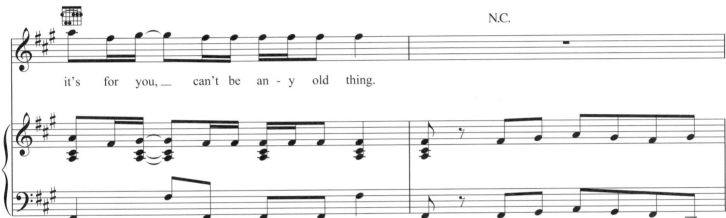

it's for you,＿ can't be an-y old thing.

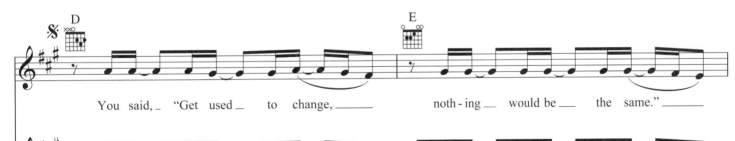

You said,＿ "Get used＿ to change,＿＿ noth-ing＿ would be＿ the same."＿＿

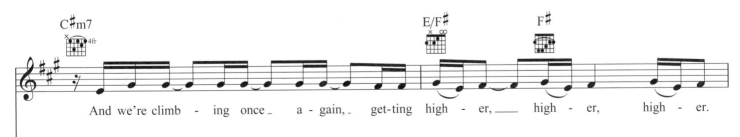

And we're climb - ing once＿ a - gain,＿ get-ting high - er,＿＿ high - er, high - er.

Stress is cruel, ___ fame's a lie ___ but you're __

__ spe - cial on ev - 'ry ___ lev - el. Suc - cess is cool, _

mon - ey is fine ___ but you're __ spe - cial, an - oth - er __

__ lev - el. If it's for you, __ can't be an - y old thing. If

it's for you, __ can't be an - y old thing. If it's for you, __ can't be an - y old thing. If

it's for you, __ can't be an - y old thing. If it's for you, __ can't be an - y old thing. If

Bm7

C#7 F#m

it's for you, __ can't be an - y old thing. If it's for you, __ can't be an - y old thing.

N.C. D.S. al Coda

CODA E/F# F#

high - er, _____ high - er, high - er.

WAVE

Words and Music by JUSTIN TIMBERLAKE,
CHAD HUGO and PHARRELL WILLIAMS

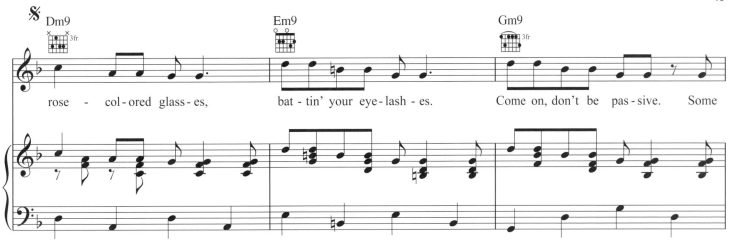

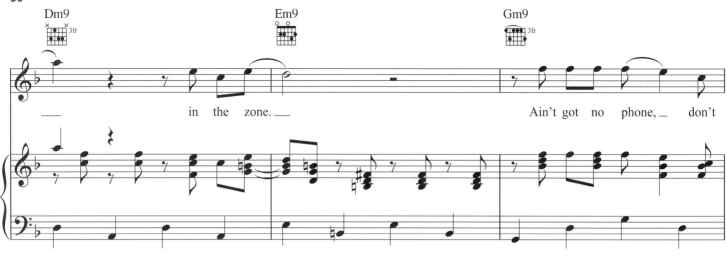

in the zone. ___ Ain't got no phone, ___ don't

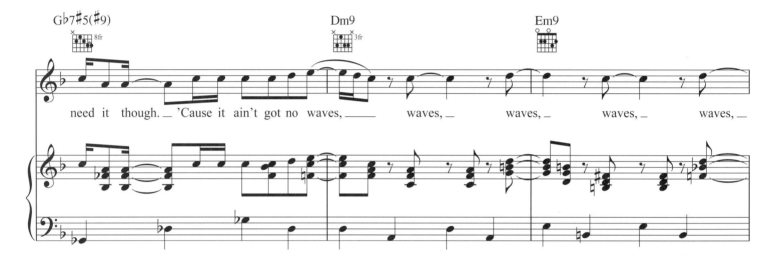

need it though. ___ 'Cause it ain't got no waves, _____ waves, _ waves, _ waves, _ waves, _

___ waves, _ waves, _ waves. ___ And just wave, _____ wave, _ wave, _

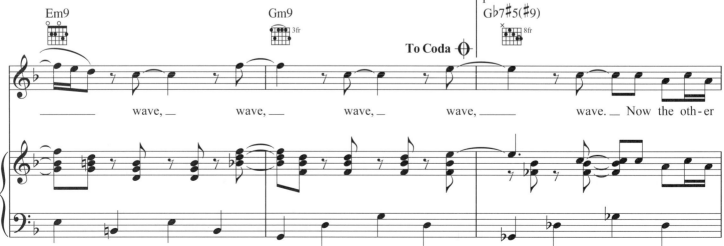

___ wave, _ wave, _ wave, _ wave, _____ wave. ___ Now the oth-er

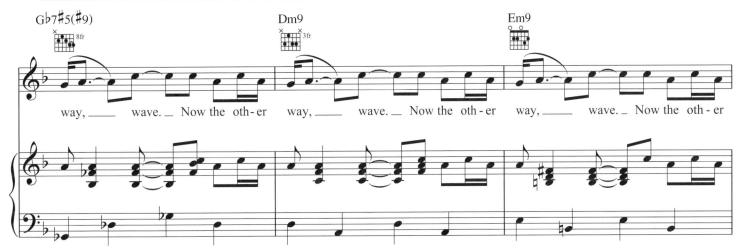

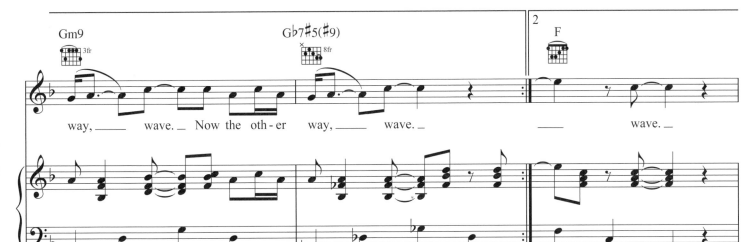

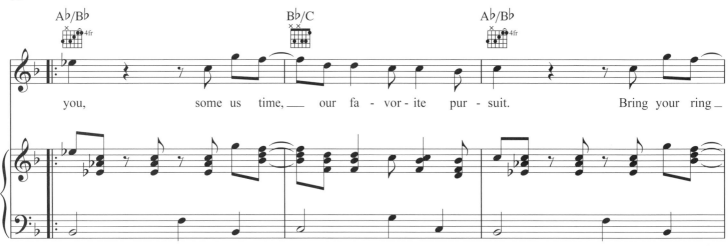

you, some us time,___ our fa - vor - ite pur - suit. Bring your ring___

___ of shades, no need for shoes. All I need___ is your skin and the

air.___ I swear to air.___

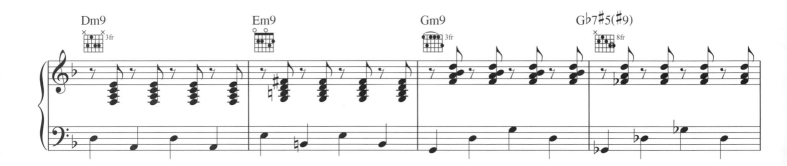

Wave, __ wave, __ wave, __ wave. __ I got on

__ wave. __ Now the oth-er way. ____ Now the oth-er way. ____ Now the oth-er

way. ____ Now the oth-er way. ____ Now the oth-er way. ____ Now the oth-er

way. ____ Now the oth-er way. ____ Now the oth-er way. ____ Wave.

SUPPLIES

Words and Music by JUSTIN TIMBERLAKE,
CHAD HUGO and PHARRELL WILLIAMS

I got you, I got sup - plie - ie - ies, (Oh, ____ oh.) ____ sup -
(Oh.) ____

To Coda

plie - ie - ies. (Oh, ____ oh.) ____ I don't know if you 'mem - ber this, but

I was out of town, ____ flew in on a three ____ a. m. just to

show up and hear your sounds. ____ The mul - ti - ple times ____

(stop) hit the set.＿ You ain't head - ed that ＿ way, I can

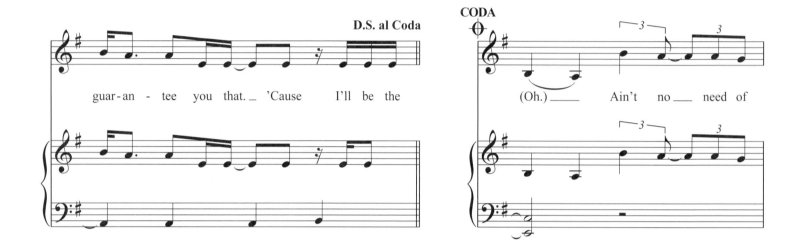

D.S. al Coda

guar - an - tee you that.＿ 'Cause I'll be the

CODA

(Oh.) ＿ Ain't no ＿ need of

stop - ping, girl. Can't no - bod - y top it, girl. Ain't no ＿ bet - ter

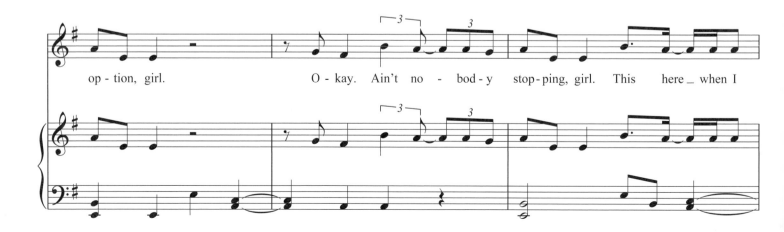

op - tion, girl. O - kay. Ain't no - bod - y stop - ping, girl. This here ＿ when I

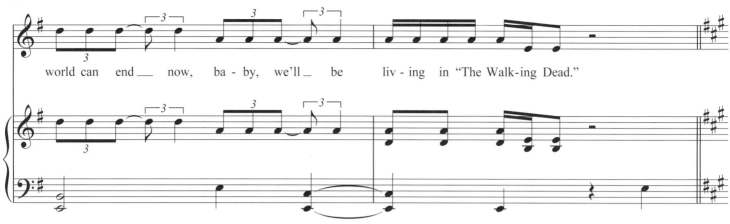

world can end __ now, ba-by, we'll __ be liv-ing in "The Walk-ing Dead."

Now, I wan-na know ev-'ry-thing; don't leave __ a

sin-gle __ de-tail out. __ I'll get __ mine lat-er, __ just swell out. __

That makes me __ a gen-er-ous lov-er. __ Ooh, __ I wan-na

see ev-'ry-thing, so don't leave_ a sin-gle_ de-tail out._

I want_ it all on_ the ta - ble,_ the per-son - al

way to... Ain't no__ need of stop-ping, girl.
(Wait.)

Yeah.

There ain't no__ need of O - kay. 'Cause I got sup-

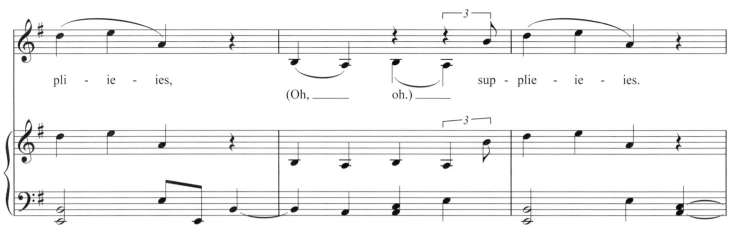

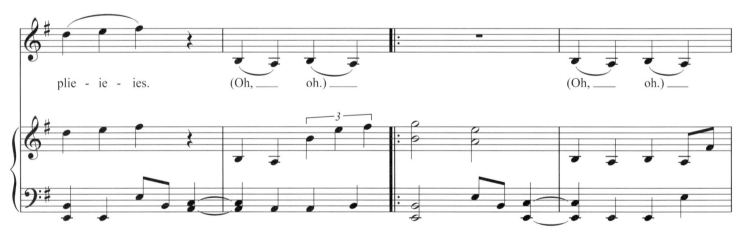

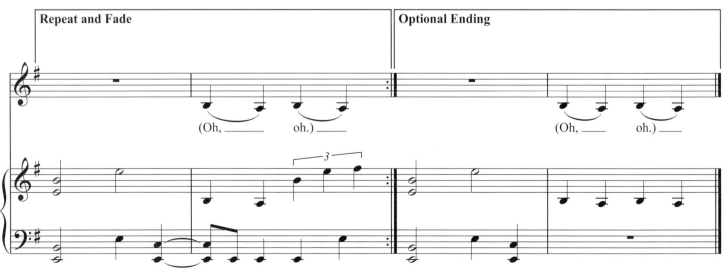

Repeat and Fade

Optional Ending

SAY SOMETHING

Words and Music by JUSTIN TIMBERLAKE,
CHRIS STAPLETON, NATE HILLS,
LARRANCE DOPSON and TIM MOSLEY

Moderately

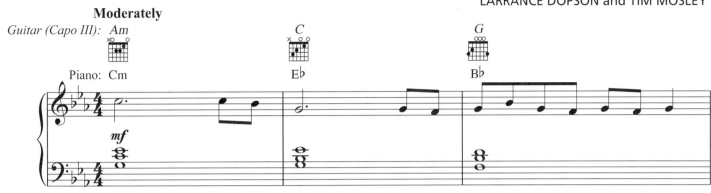

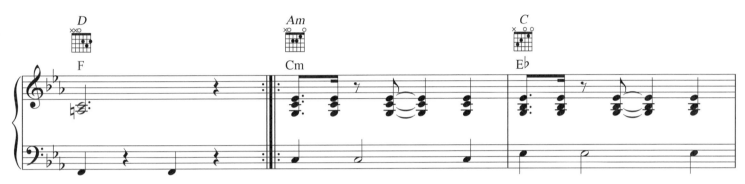

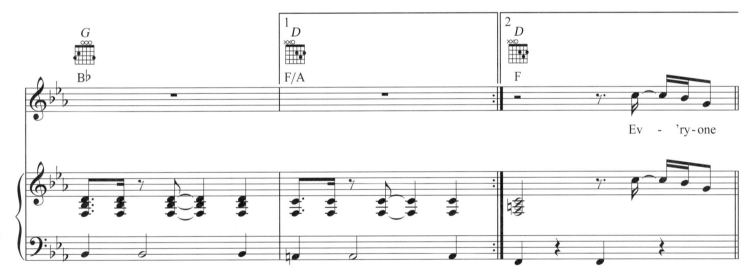

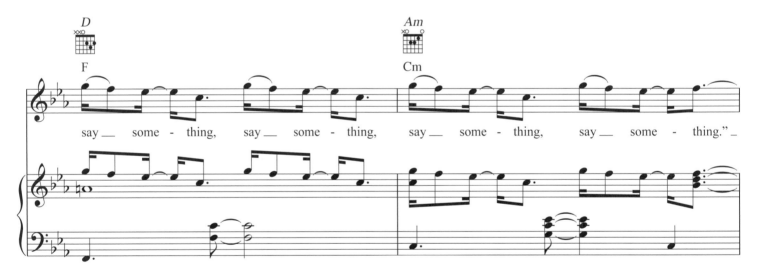

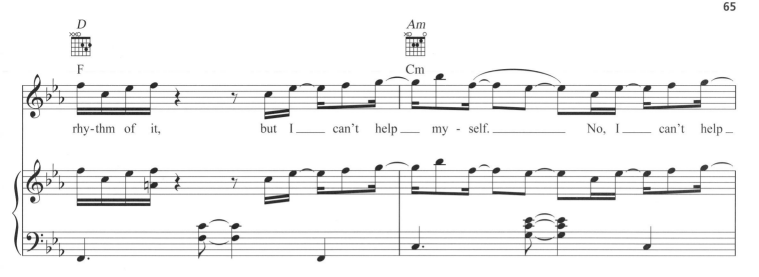

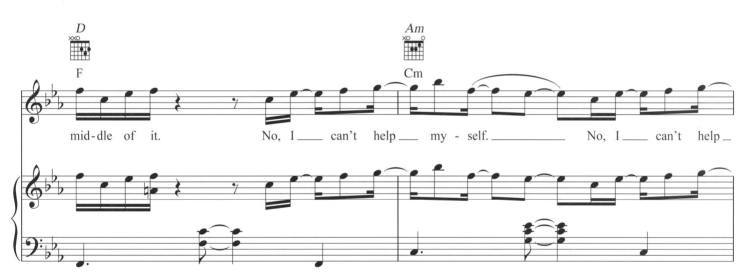

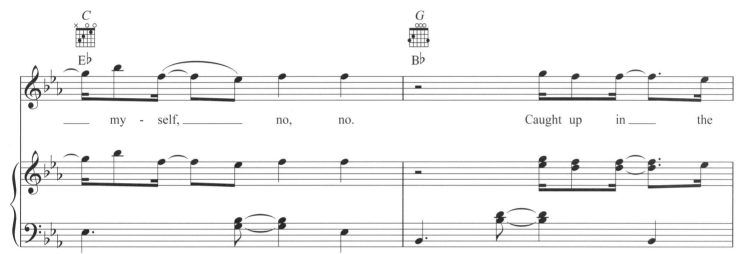

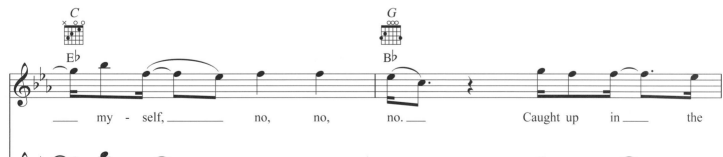

har - mo - ny for you and me to - night. _____

Am
Cm
C
Eb

D.S. al Coda

I hear ___ them call ___ my name. ___ Ev - 'ry - bod - y says,

G
Bb
D
F

CODA

- thing I ___ can't ___ have. May-be I'm look-ing for some-

Am
Cm
C
Eb

- thing I ___ can't have. ___ May-be I'm look-ing for some-

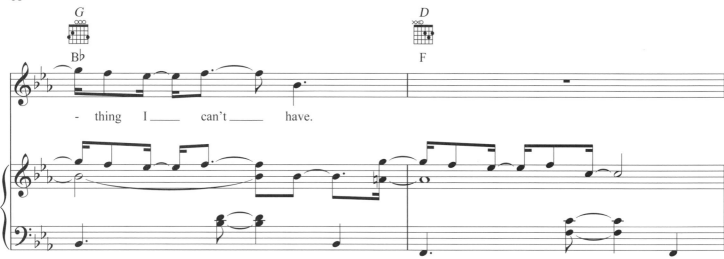

- thing I can't have.

Some - times the great -

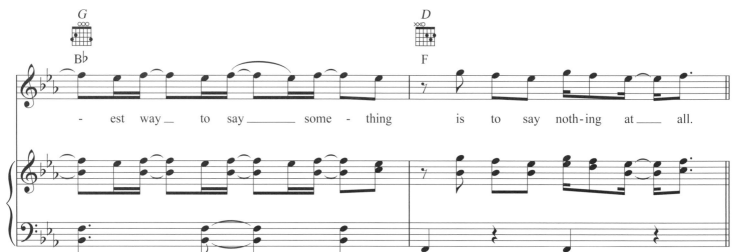

- est way to say some - thing is to say noth-ing at all.

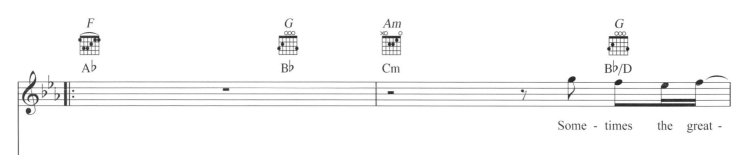

Some - times the great -

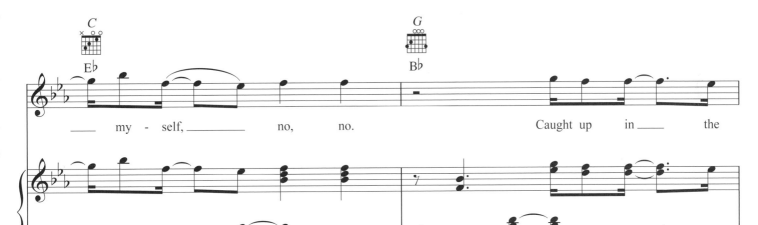

May-be I'm look-ing for some - thing I ___ can't ___ have.

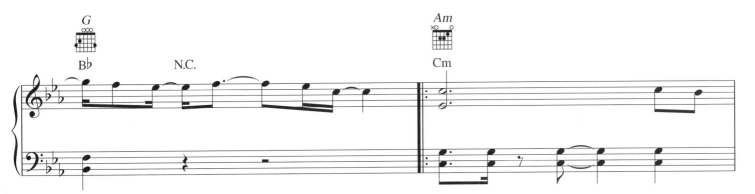

Some-times the great - est way ___ to say _____ some - thing

is to say noth-ing at ___ all.   is to say noth-ing.

MORNING LIGHT

Words and Music by JUSTIN TIMBERLAKE,
CHRIS STAPLETON, ERIC HUDSON,
ROBIN TADROSS and ELLIOTT IVES

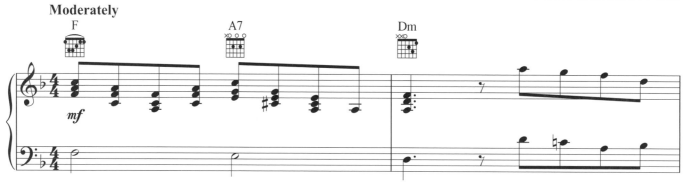

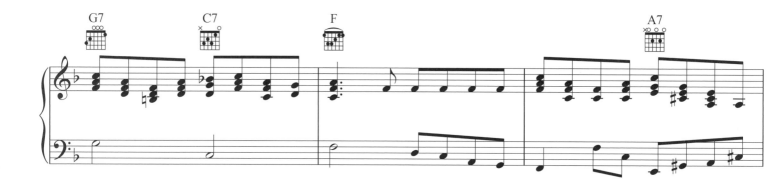

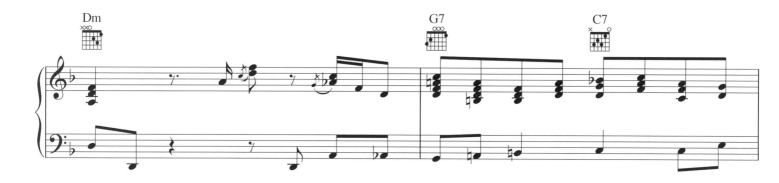

Look,   ev-'ry time there's new _____ sun - rise _____
I can't e - ven get out _____ of   bed, _____

I o - pen up my __ eyes, __
with the thoughts you're put - ting in my __ head. __

and I say to my - self, __ "In the whole wide world of guys __
So I say to my - self, __ "I don't e - ven wan - na try. __

I must be the luck - i - est __ a - live." __
Yeah, __ ev - 'ry part of me is par - a - lyzed." __

'Cause I'm in love with you, __
'Cause I'm in love with you, __

lay - ing here ____ in the morn - ing light. ____
lay - ing here ____ in he morn - ing light. ____

And all I wan - na do ____
And all I wan - na do ____

is hold you tight ____ just one more ____ night. ____
is hold you tight ____ just one more ____ night. ____

Look, ____ Yes, I'm in love with

you, _____ lay - ing here _

___ in the morn - ing light. ___ And all I wan - na

do _____ is hold you tight _

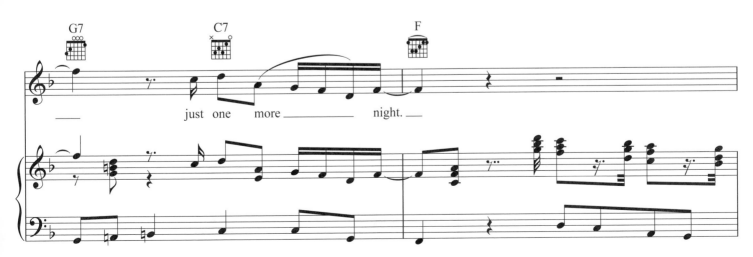

___ just one more _____ night. ___

do, _____ just hold you tight _

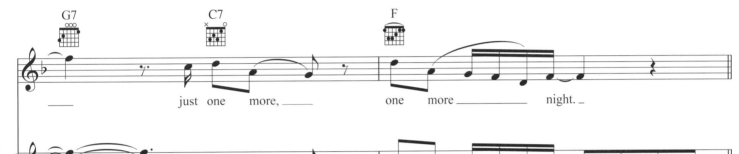

just one more, _____ one more _____ night. _

Repeat and Fade   **Optional Ending**

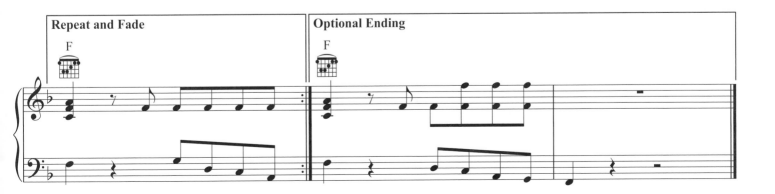

HERS
(Interlude)

Words and Music by
JUSTIN TIMBERLAKE

Flowing

(See spoken text)

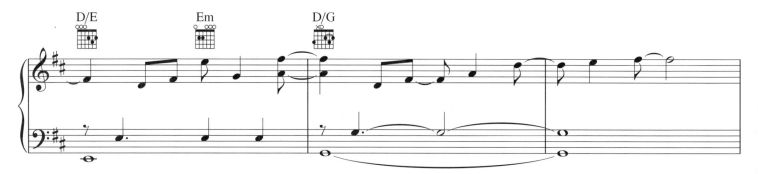

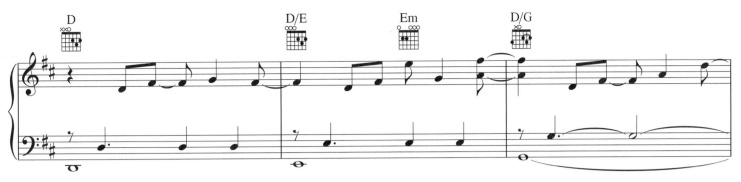

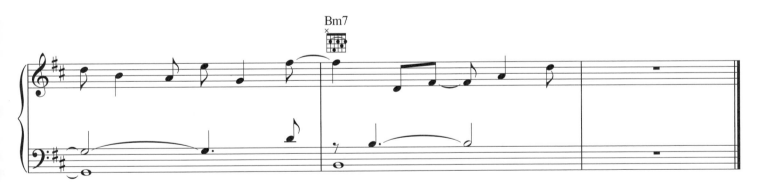

Spoken:

When I wear his shirt, it feels like, like his skin over mine. And the little holes and tears and shreds on it are, are, are the, the memories of the past that I wasn't there for, but, that somehow I, I, I feel like I understand more when it's against my skin. It's an armor, like a barrier from the world. Like, our secret nobody else knows and I like that, you know? It makes me feel like a woman, it makes me feel sexy, it makes me feel... it makes me feel like I'm his.

FLANNEL

Words and Music by JUSTIN TIMBERLAKE,
CHAD HUGO and PHARRELL WILLIAMS

Acoustic Ballad

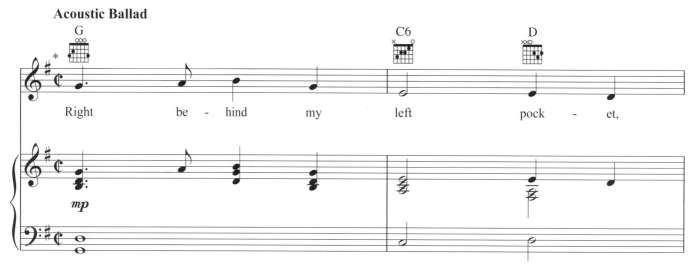

Right be-hind my left pock-et,

that is where you'll feel my soul. It's been with me

man-y win-ters, it will keep you warm.

* Recorded a half-step lower

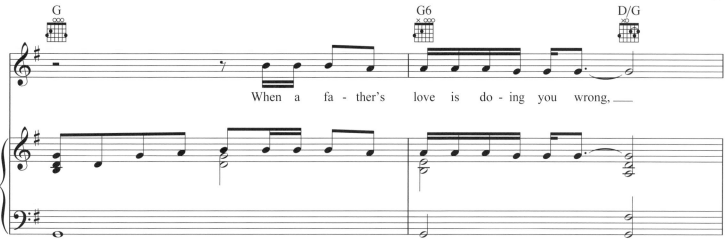

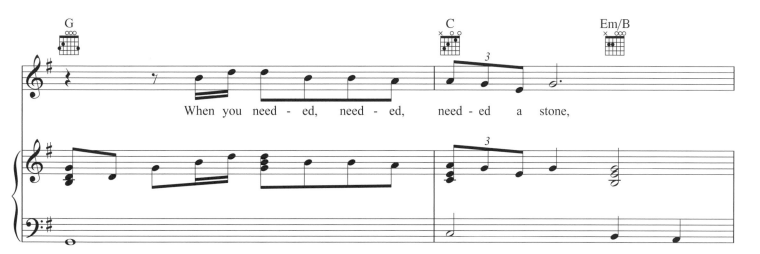

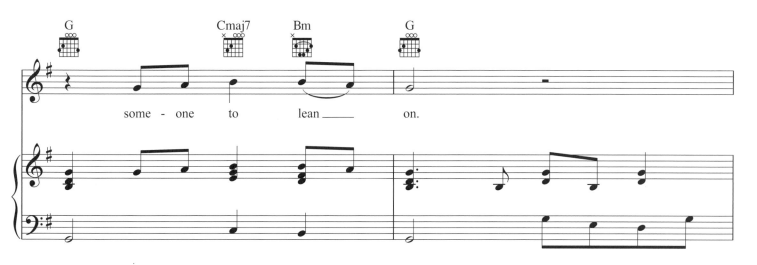

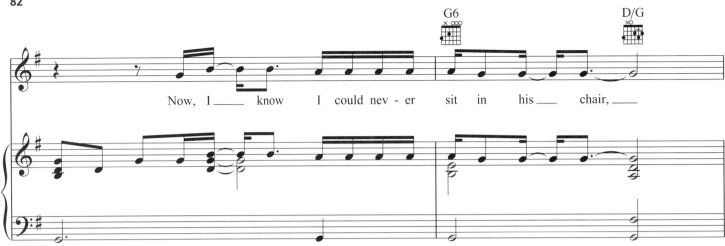

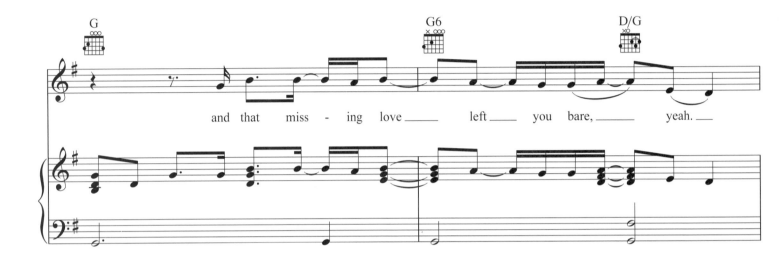

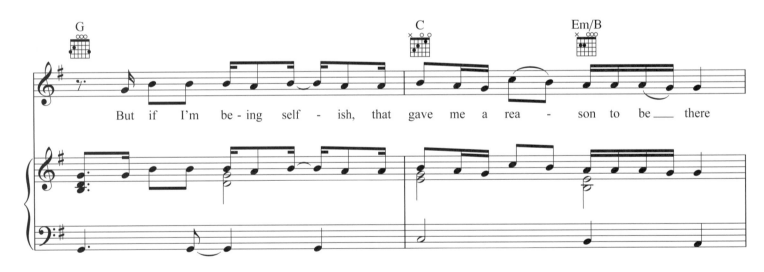

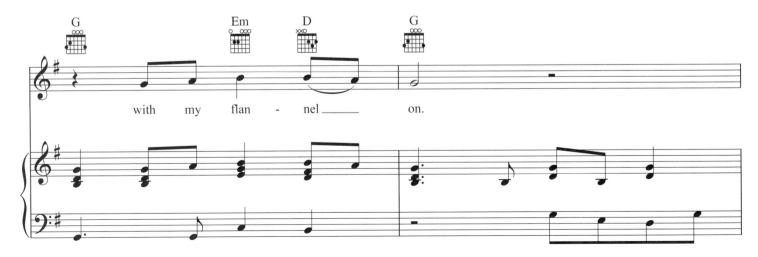

Right be-hind my left pock-et, that is where you'll

feel my soul. It's been with me man-y win-ters,

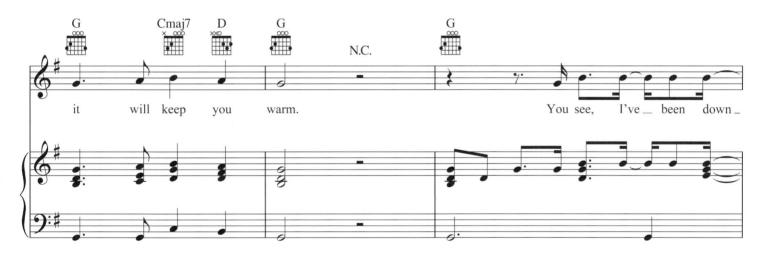

it will keep you warm. You see, I've been down

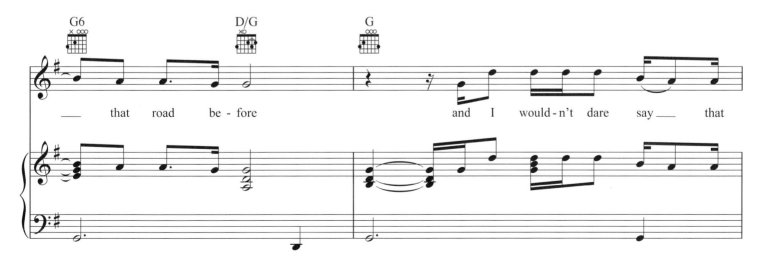

that road be-fore and I would-n't dare say that

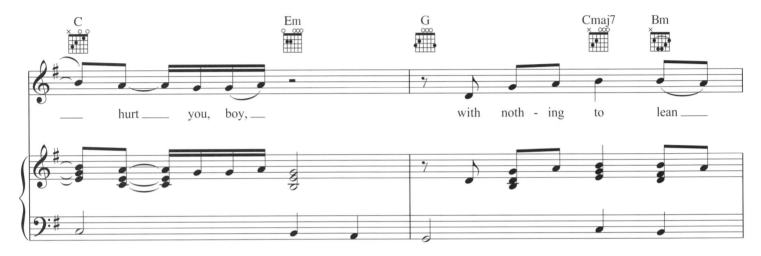

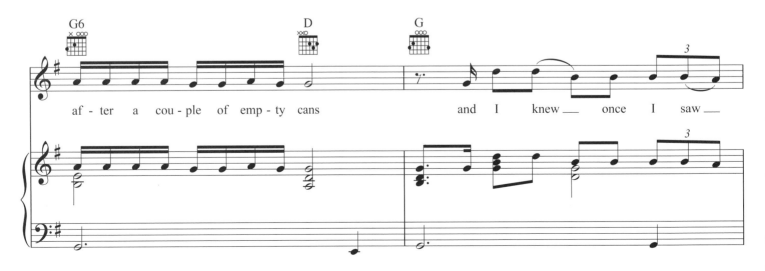

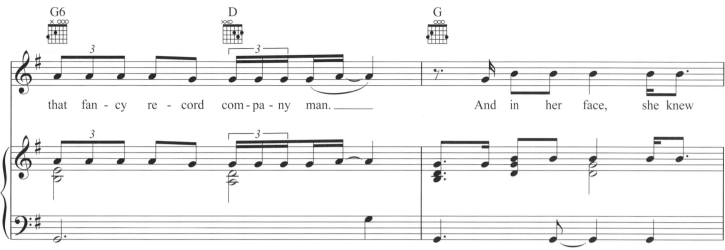

that fan-cy re-cord com-pa-ny man. _____ And in her face, she knew

I was-n't stay-ing, _ I was leav-ing with my flan-nel ___ on.

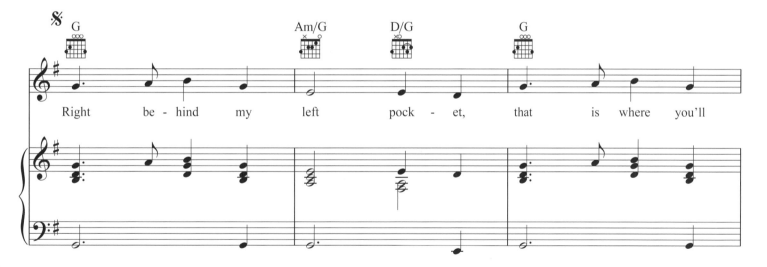

Right be-hind my left pock - et, that is where you'll

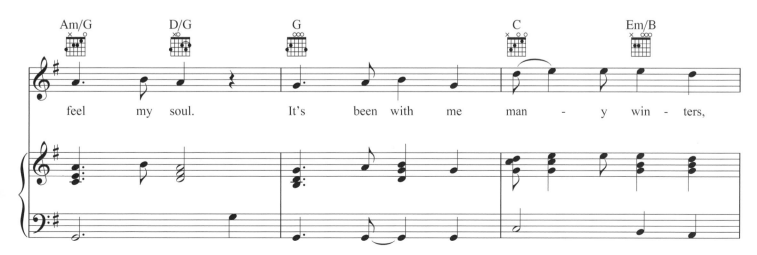

feel my soul. It's been with me man - y win - ters,

it will keep you warm. The char - ac - ter's in the

way you wear it, it takes your shape while you keep it on.

To Coda ⊕

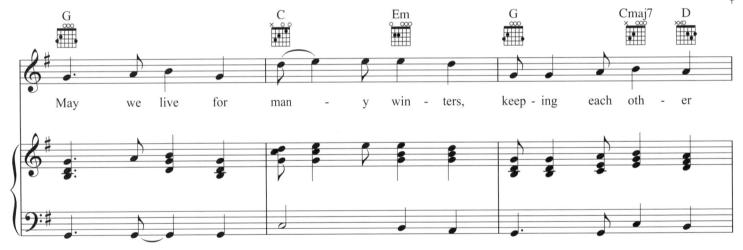

May we live for man - y win - ters, keep - ing each oth - er

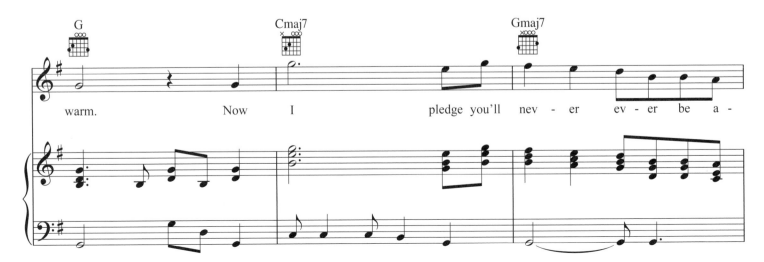

warm. Now I pledge you'll nev - er ev - er be a -

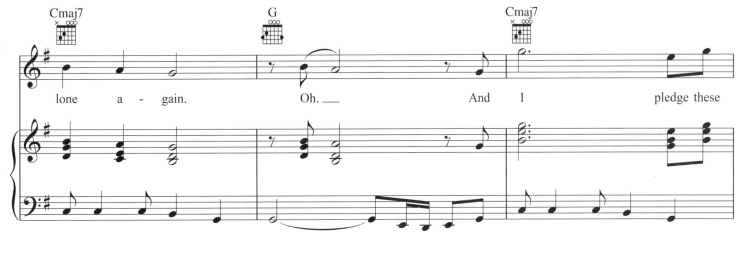

lone a - gain. Oh. ___ And I pledge these

D.S. al Coda

arms and chest are here to hold ___ you ___ in from the cold. _____

CODA

warm. And may we live for

man - y win - ters, keep - ing each oth - er warm.

MONTANA

Words and Music by JUSTIN TIMBERLAKE,
CHAD HUGO and PHARRELL WILLIAMS

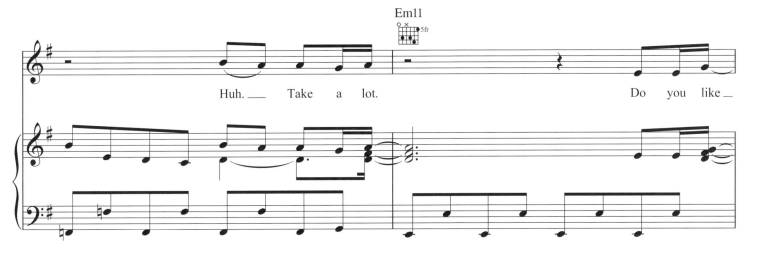

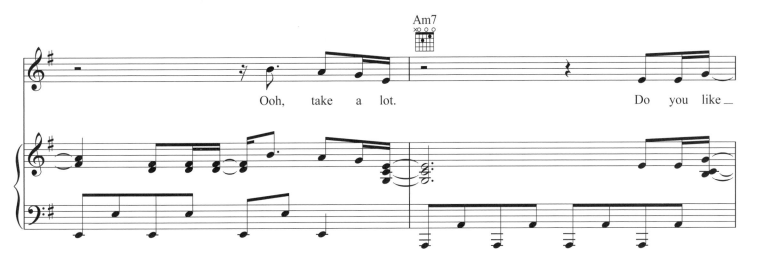

To Coda

that you can have __ it all. ____

(Take what-

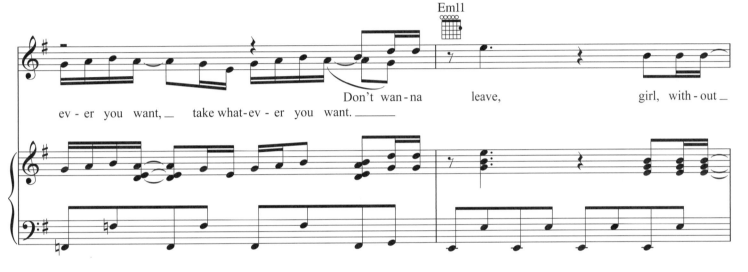

ev - er you want, __ take what-ev - er you want. _____

Don't wan-na leave, __ girl, with-out __

____ you. And I can't sleep, no, I would-n't know how __

____ to. When I need a com - pass, yeah __ (yeah), __

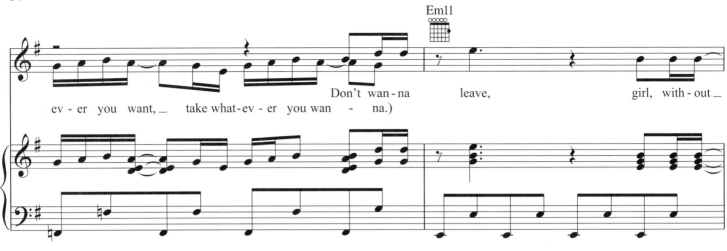

Don't wan-na leave, girl, with-out ev-er you want, _ take what-ev-er you wan - na.)

_ you. And I can't sleep, no, I would-n't know how _ _ to.

When I need a com - pass, yeah _ (yeah), _

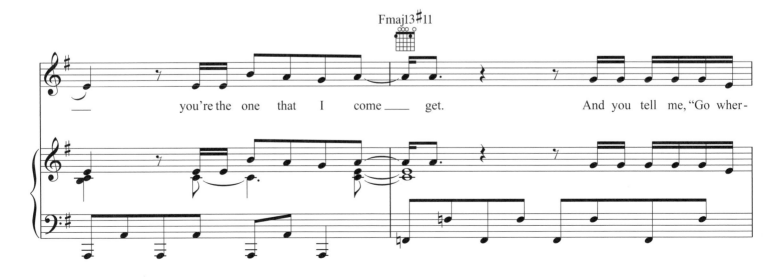

you're the one that I come _ get. And you tell me, "Go wher-

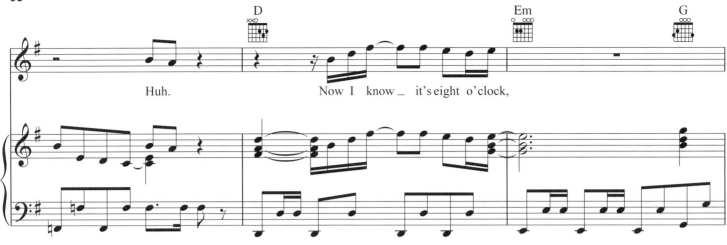

Huh.

Now I know ___ it's eight o'clock,

and we've ___ been kiss-ing for hours. ___

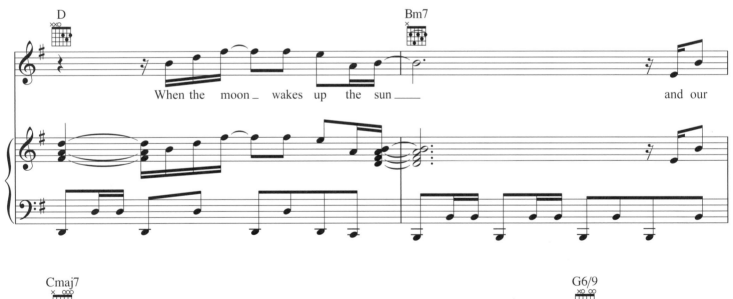

When the moon ___ wakes up the sun ___ and our

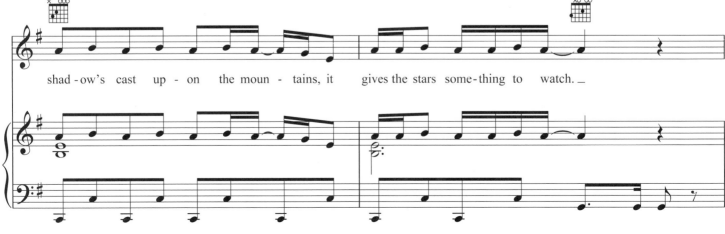

shad-ow's cast up-on the moun-tains, it gives the stars some-thing to watch. ___

Yes, I know it's eight o'-clock, ___ yeah, oh, ___

and we've_ been kiss-ing for hours; _____

but when the moon_ wakes up the sun ___ and our

D.S. al Coda

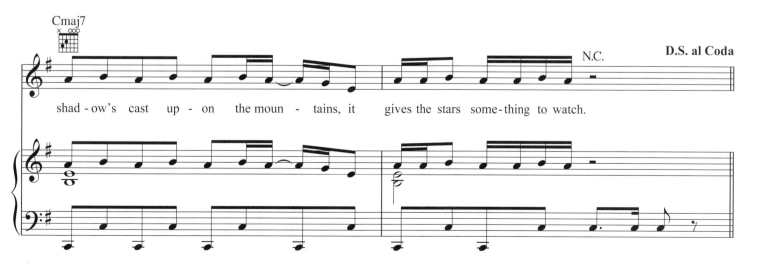

shad-ow's cast up-on the moun-tains, it gives the stars some-thing to watch.

BREEZE OFF THE POND

Words and Music by JUSTIN TIMBERLAKE,
CHAD HUGO and PHARRELL WILLIAMS

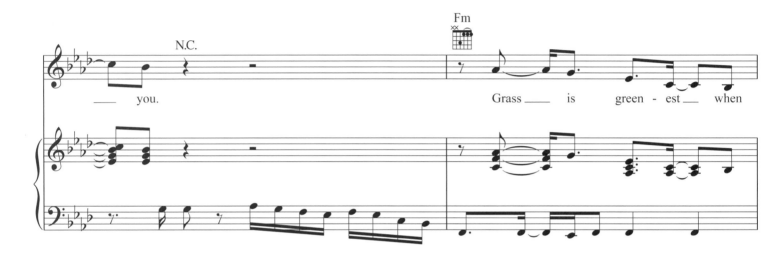

good _____ then why would _ they _____ trade? Mmm.

Now, we are in the zone _ and we
Huff and puff all they want, _ but this

ain't gon-na let it go, _____ no way. _____
house is-n't made of straw _ or clay. _____

What we got is sol-id as oak, _ so you

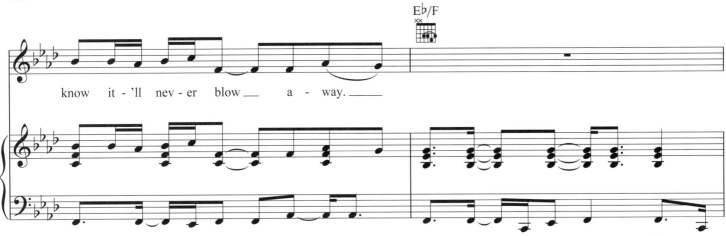

know it -'ll nev-er blow ___ a - way. ___

Uh, like breeze off ___ the pond ___

___ or trees on ___ the lawn. ___

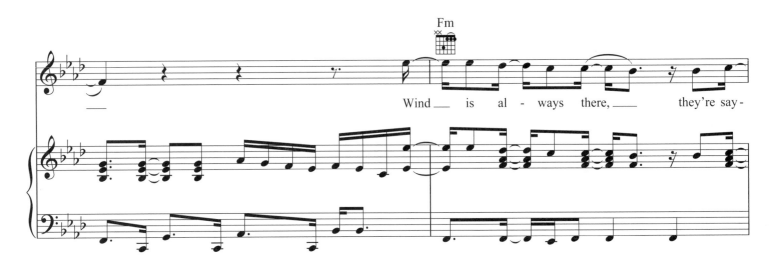

Wind ___ is al - ways there, ___ they're say-

To Coda ⊕

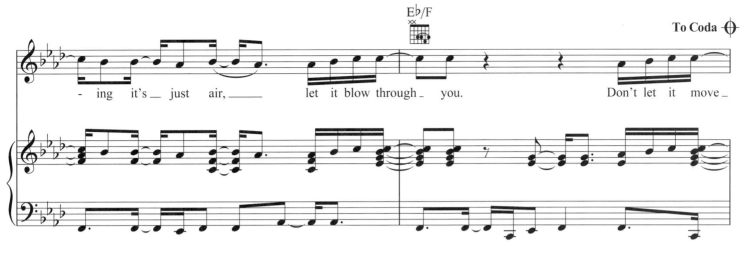

- ing it's __ just air, _____ let it blow through __ you. Don't let it move __

__ you. Now __ the __ sun danc - es __ a -

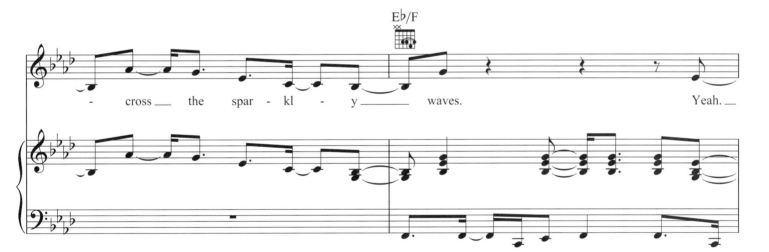

- cross __ the spar - kl - y _____ waves. Yeah. __

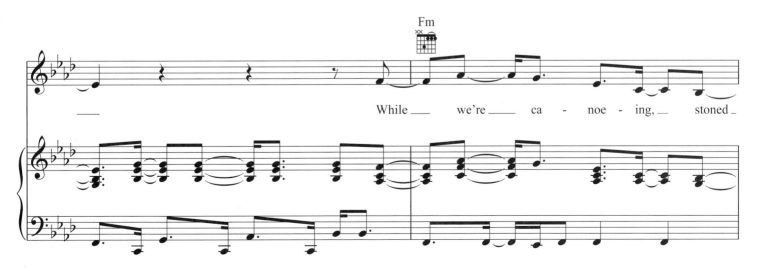

__ While __ we're __ ca - noe - ing, __ stoned __

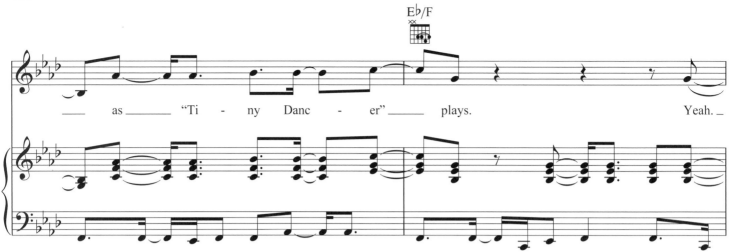

as _____ "Ti - ny Danc - er" _____ plays. Yeah. _

_____ you.

Like breeze off __ the pond _

or trees on __ the lawn. _

Wind _

is al - ways there, ___ they're say - ing it's ___ just air, ___ let it blow through

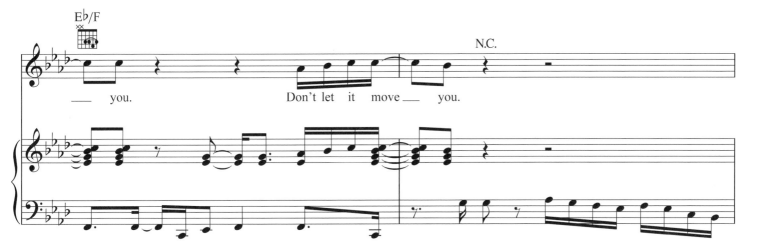

___ you. Don't let it move ___ you.

You and I ___ a - gainst the world, ___ 'gainst the world, ___ 'gainst the world. ___

___ You and I ___ a - gainst the world ___ and ev - 'ry - thing it comes with.

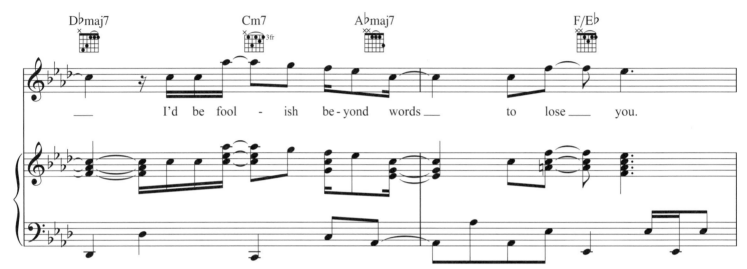

Dᵇmaj7　　　Cm7　　　Aᵇmaj7

What I'd look like try'n' to hide my life,　one of those guys, I was taught you should keep it low. _

Dᵇmaj7　　　Cm7　　　Aᵇmaj7

1

N.C.

_ Nuh - uh, want a bill-board space with a big old sign you could see from the high-way.

2

N.C.

Uh, like breeze off _ the pond. _ big old sign you could see from the high-way.

THE HARD STUFF

Words and Music by JUSTIN TIMBERLAKE,
CHRIS STAPLETON, ERIC HUDSON,
ROBIN TADROSS and ELLIOTT IVES

So give me the hard ___ stuff ___ (hard stuff). ___

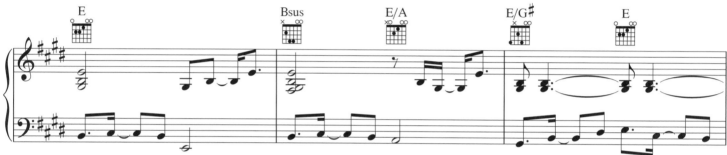

An-y-bod-y who can be in love ___ on a
But God ___ knows ___ I'm ___ not the man ___ that I

sun-ny day,
wan-na be.
and an-y-bod-y who can turn and run ___ when it
And we all ___ know ___ there's things in this life we re-

starts to rain, __
fuse to see. __
and ev-'ry-bod-y wish-es all their skies were
So just __ know __ my fire for you will

blue; _____
al-ways burn; __
but that ain't __ the kind __ of love __ I'm look-ing to
and __ please __ for-give __ the things __ in this life that I

have with you. __ }
have to learn. __ }
So give me the hard __ stuff, __ the kind that makes you

real. _____
I'll be there when the storm __ comes, 'cause I want the hard __

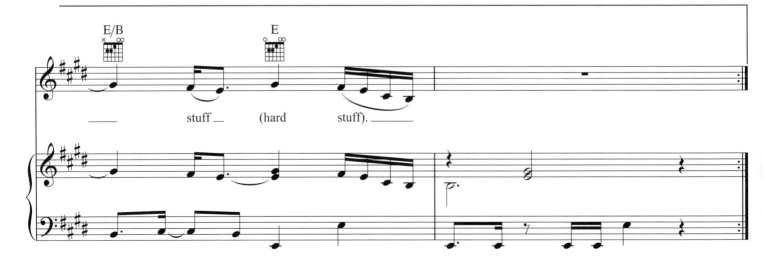

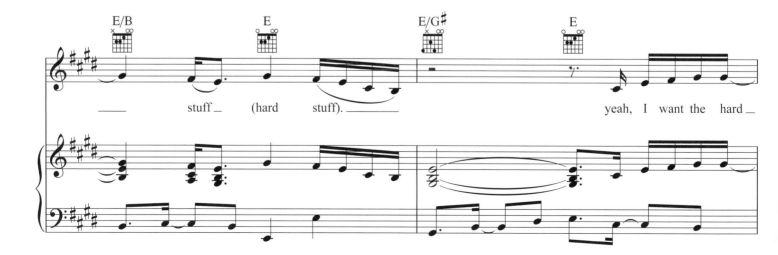

YOUNG MAN

Words and Music by JUSTIN TIMBERLAKE,
JAMES FAUNTLEROY, JEROME HARMON
and TIMOTHY MOSLEY

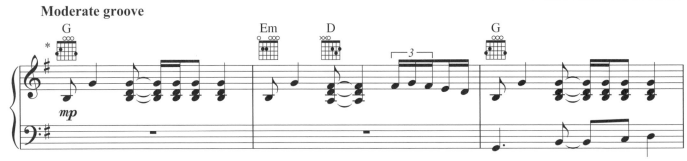

Lyrics:
I said, young man. Sit down, let me tell you how it's s'posed to be.___ How they told me.___ Said, young man.___ If you wan-na make God smile,___ make plans.___ You've got___ to be rea-dy.___

Recorded a half step lower than written.

You don't un-der-stand, __ right now __ you're a young man.

To Coda

You gon' have __ to stand __ for some-thin'. Beau-ti-ful boy, __ got it from your ma-ma.

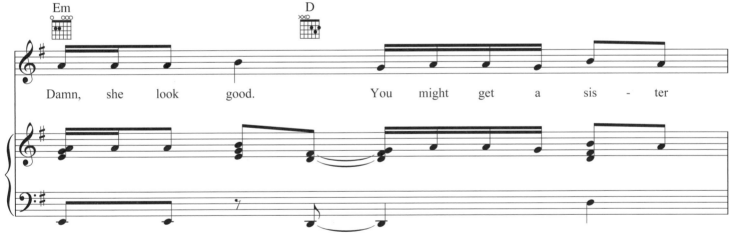

Damn, she look good. You might get a sis-ter

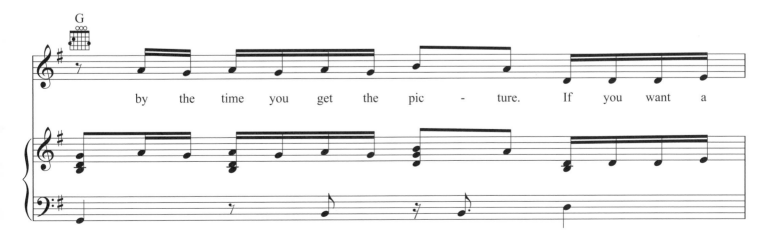

by the time you get the pic-ture. If you want a

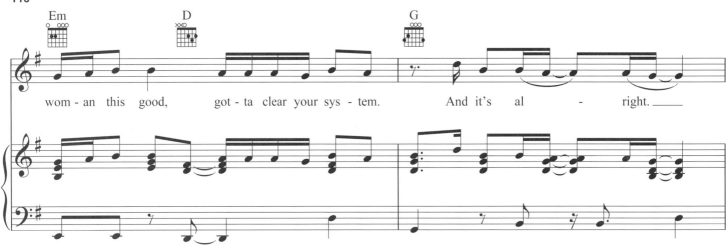

woman this good, gotta clear your system. And it's al - right.____

If you need to cry, you've got my per-mis-sion. You can do an-y-thing__ in the

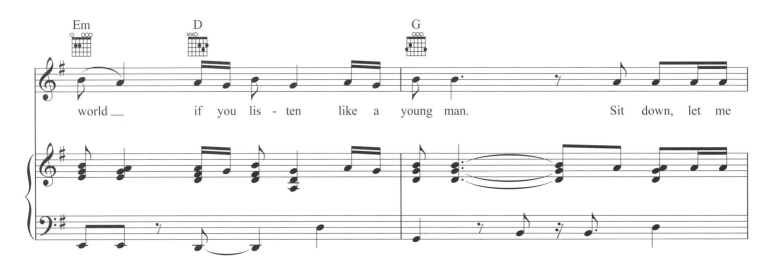

world__ if you lis-ten like a young man. Sit down, let me

tell you how it's s'posed to be.__ How they told me.__ Said, young man.__ If you wan-na

make God smile _____ make plans._____ You've got___ to be rea-dy._____

You don't un-der-stand,___ right now___ you're a young man. But

you gon' have___ to stand___ for some-thin'. We don't ev-er back down, don't back down.

We don't have to act out, don't act out. And ev-en when you fall, don't stay down.

If you need me a-round, you know I stay down. _____ And an-y-where you go, _____

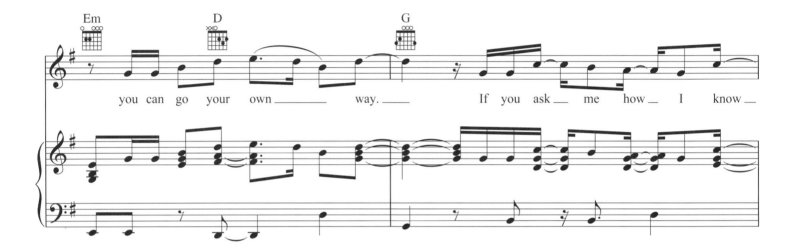

you can go your own _____ way. ____ If you ask__ me how__ I know__

___ these things, _ re-mem-ber I once__ was a young man. Sit down, let me

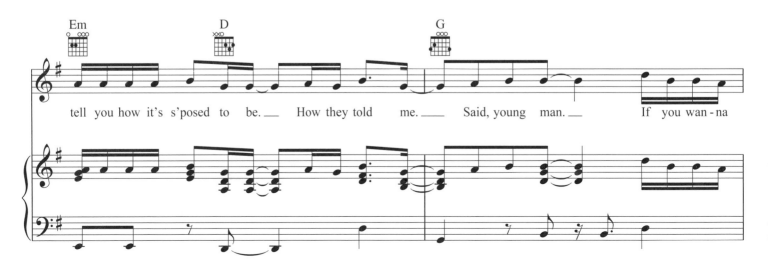

tell you how it's s'posed to be. __ How they told me. __ Said, young man. __ If you wan-na

make God smile, _____ make plans. _____ You've got_ to be rea - dy. _____

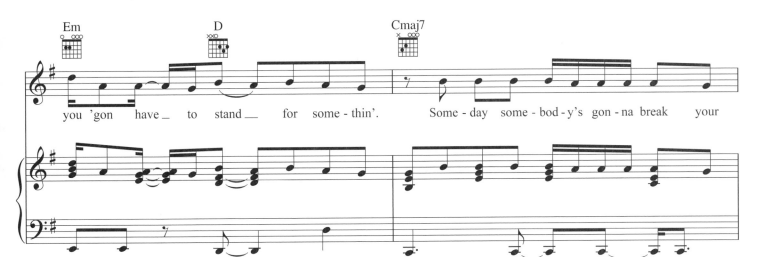

You don't un - der - stand, _ right now _ you're a young man. But

you 'gon have _ to stand _ for some - thin'. Some - day some - bod - y's gon - na break your

heart in two and I'll be there. Some - day you're gon - na break some - bod - y's

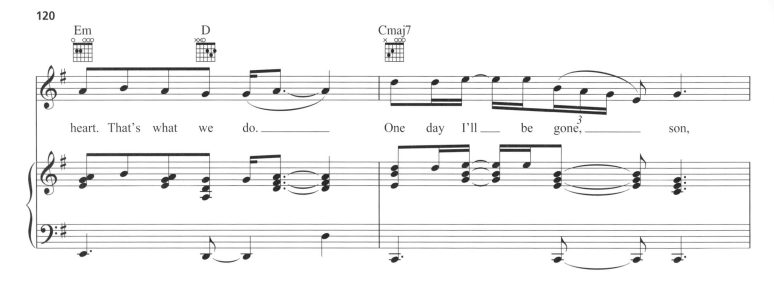

heart. That's what we do. _____ One day I'll __ be gone, _____ son,

but right now __ I'm home. __ No, __ you'll nev - er be __ a - lone. _____ May - be

some - day you'll __ be talk - in' to ____ your own young man, yeah. __

You know your dad-dy's so proud of you, __ my lit - tle young man. _____

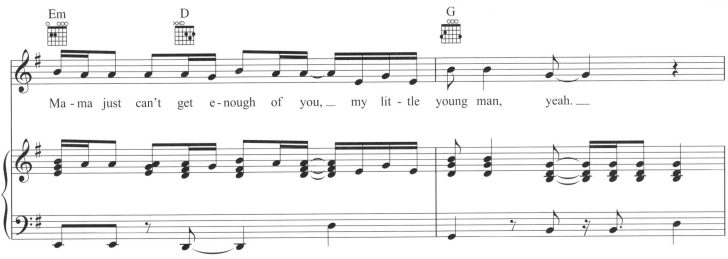

Ma - ma just can't get e - nough of you, __ my lit - tle young man, yeah. __

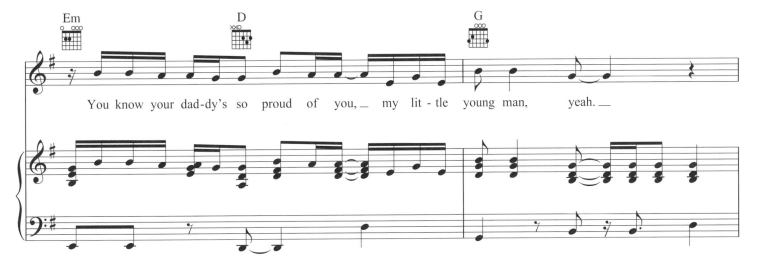

You know your dad - dy's so proud of you, __ my lit - tle young man, yeah. __

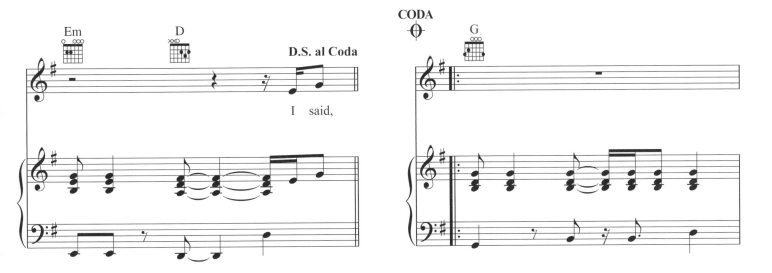

D.S. al Coda

I said,

CODA

Optional Ending

Repeat and Fade

LIVIN' OFF THE LAND

Words and Music by JUSTIN TIMBERLAKE,
CHAD HUGO and PHARRELL WILLIAMS

Sun - day, you're goin' to church; back on your knees, and you're try'n' to soul search, sing-ing,

"I'm just one man, _____ do-ing ___ the best ___ that I

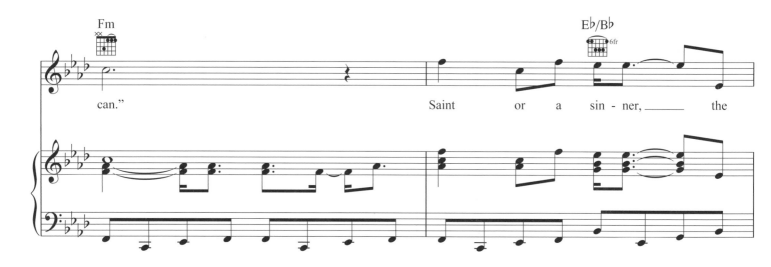

can." Saint or a sin - ner, _____ the

los - er can be a win - ner with a plan

To Coda 🖌

D.S. al Coda

liv-in' off __ the land. __

CODA

when you're liv-in' off __ the land, ____

1st time only:

liv-in' off __ the land. __

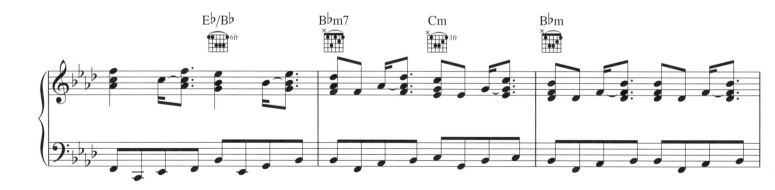

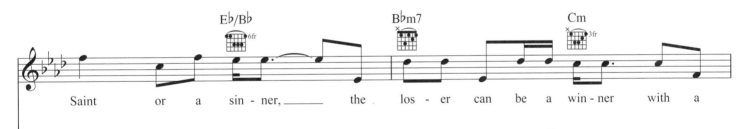

If you just o-pen up your-self, (If you just

o-pen up your-self,) if you just o-pen up your-self, (if you just

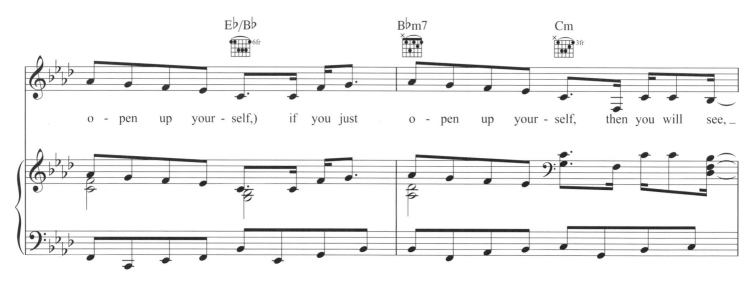

o-pen up your-self,) if you just o-pen up your-self, then you will see, __

__ got what you need __ when you're liv-in' off __ the land. __